Who Am I?

Friendly and not so friendly Faces of the Desert

BY **SUE HAWKINS**   ILLUSTRATED BY **KELLY NOGOSKI**

First published by Experience Early Learning Company
7243 Scotchwood Lane, Grawn, Michigan 49637 USA

Text Copyright ©2016 by Experience Early Learning Co.
Printed and Bound in the USA

ISBN 978-1-937954-30-7
visit us at **www.ExperienceEarlyLearning.com**

I have wings
and I am small
enough to sit
in your hands.

Who am I?

2

I am
a cactus
pygmy owl.

Find my yellow eyes that
don't seem to blink.

Can you open your eyes wide
without blinking and count to 10?

I have spiny armor
on my back
and a long tail.

Who am I?

I am an armadillo lizard.

Find the scales on my protective armor.

Can you roll into a ball like a scared armadillo lizard? Protect your soft belly.

I have soft fur like a pet cat, but I am much bigger and stronger. Who am I?

I am a bobcat.

Find my pointed ears.

Lick your paws and make
a ferocious growling sound.

I have eight legs and front pincers called pedipalps. Who am I?

I am a scorpion.

Find my segmented tail and count my legs.

Can you lie on your stomach and pinch your hands like pedipalps?

I don't have a tail
and can live
in the water
or on land.
Who am I?

19

I am
a desert toad.

Find my dry, warty skin.

Hop like a toad
and then pretend to sleep
for the winter.

I can match
my color
to the ground
where I stand.
Who am I?

I am
a thorny dragon.

Find the knob on my back.

Puff up your cheeks and body
to look bigger than you are
and scare away a predator.

I have a hard shell and long claws to dig my burrow home. Who am I?

I am a desert tortoise.

Find my nose and mouth covered in leathery skin.

Pretend to wear a heavy shell and crawl around the room.

I roam the desert looking for shade and food. I have a snout and tusks.

Who am I?

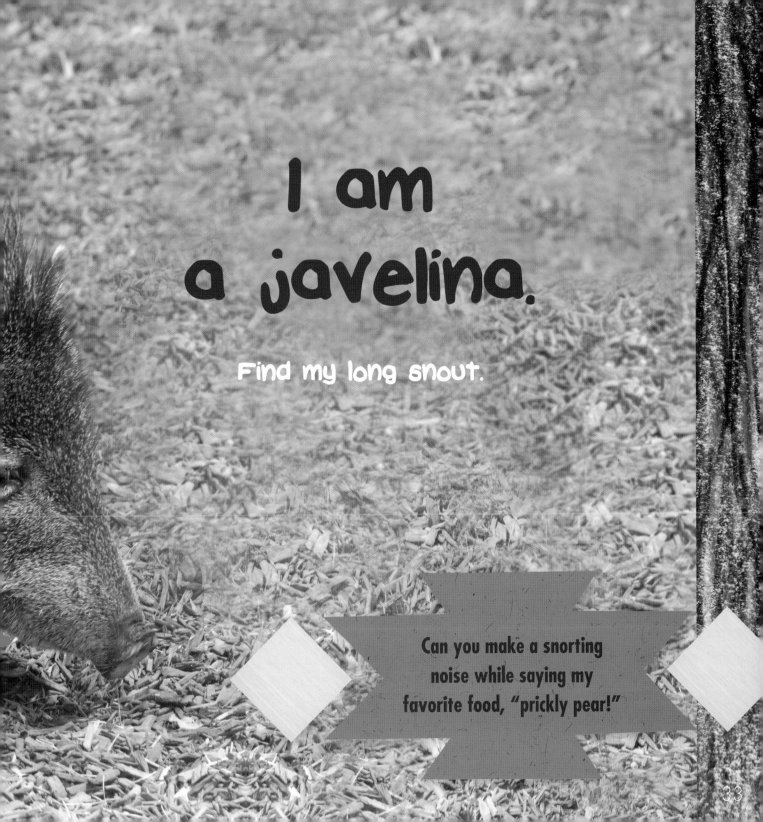

I am
a javelina.

Find my long snout.

Can you make a snorting
noise while saying my
favorite food, "prickly pear!"

I am four feet long but have no legs. I can be very dangerous. Who am I?

I am a Mojave rattlesnake.

Find the diamond shapes on my back.

Slither on the ground
and show your sharp,
scary teeth.

I am very
smart and clever.
I have
pointed ears
and a bushy tail.
Who am I?

I am a coyote.

Find my eyes. What do you think I see?

Raise your head and howl.
Then, sit very still like
a watchful coyote.

I have very large, furry ears and a tiny little face.
Who am I?

I am
a desert fox.

Find my large, pointed ears.

Swing your hips and shake
your large, pointed ears.

I look like a horse, but I have longer ears and a shorter mane. Who am I?

I am
a wild burro.

Find the short mane between my ears
and down my neck.

Pretend to be a burro and carry
something on your back.
Don't let it fall!

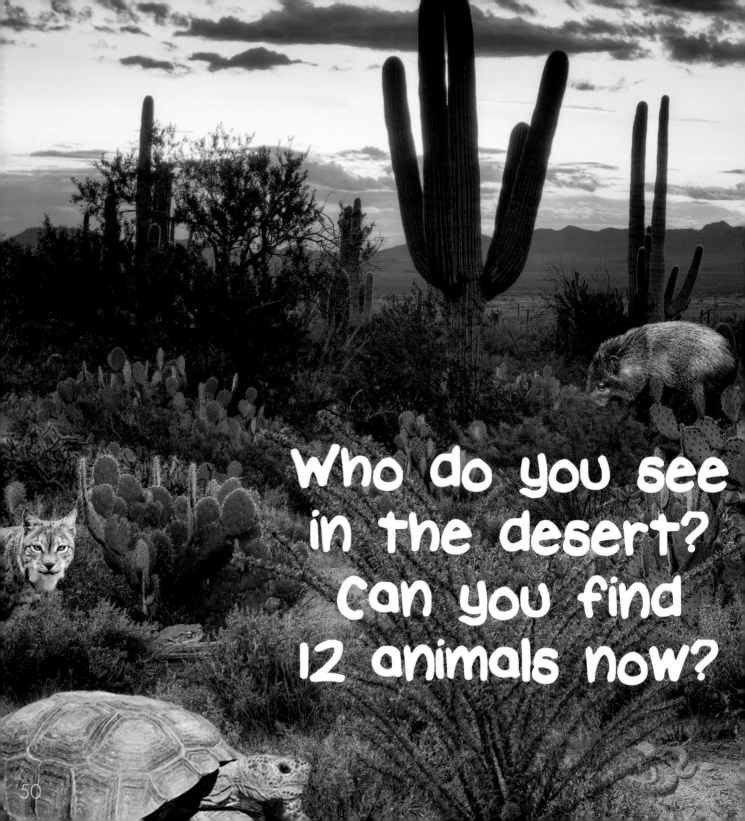

Who do you see in the desert? Can you find 12 animals now?

Guess who

1

I live in a nest in a cactus.
I have 2 round yellow eyes.
I am hatched from an egg.
Who am I?

2

I have long claws to build my burrow.
I have a shell on my back.
I live to be 80 years old.
Who am I?

3

I have dry, warty skin and no tail.
I move by hopping.
I lay 8,000 eggs in the water.
Who am I?

4

I am a member of the cat family.
My fur has many colors and helps me to hide.
I hide in the bushes to stay cool.
Who am I?

5

I have 4 short, strong legs.
I like to hide in the cracks between the rocks.
My body has spiny armor to keep me safe.
Who am I?

6

I have big ears that help me stay cool.
My feet are furry, so I don't burn them in the hot sand.
I live in an underground den.
Who am I?

Answers: 1. 2. 3. 4. 5. 6.

I Am

7

I am a furry, fast runner.
My babies are called pups and I teach them to howl.
They say I am a good problem solver and clever.
Who am I?

8

I do not have any legs but can move very fast.
Watch out for my dangerous bite.
I hide in the hot sun and go out at night.
Who am I?

9

I have 2 tusks and 3 toes on my back legs.
I eat cacti, grass, berries, and mushrooms.
I am always on the lookout for water and shade.
Who am I?

10

I have rough skin and a knob on my neck.
I eat ants one at a time and I eat 3,000 ants in one day!
I can puff up my body to look bigger and change colors.
Who am I?

11

I can walk safely on rocky ground with my 4 legs.
I look like a horse with long ears and a short mane.
I can walk for a long time without water.
Who am I?

12

I have eight legs and can pinch.
Be careful, I have dangerous venom in my tail.
I can move very quickly and surprise you!
Who am I?

7.   8.   9.  10.   11.   12.